Totally inaccessible to anything
but the narrowest of audiences
Not in any way related to
DW's interests in writing and
the exemption on the Warm Country.
Books must be in English!

EM Forster — "DW believes in
warmth — Knows that human beings
are not statues but contain flesh
+ blood + a heart

THIS MAKES A BREAK & FILLS IT. NO GARDEN
GUARDS ME. THE PERIMETER IS PIERCED.

THIS BREAKS ME & THEN FILLS ME,
SHY & VIOLENT AS IT IS.

AHSAHTA PRESS + BOISE, IDAHO + 2017

THE NEW SERIES + #84

~~FLUNG~~ THRONE

CODY-ROSE CLEVIDENCE

Ahsahta Press, Boise State University, Boise, Idaho 83725-1545
Cover design by Quemadura
Book design by Janet Holmes
ahsahtapress.org

LIBRARY OF CONGRESS CATALOGING-IN-PUBLICATION DATA

Names: Clevidence, Cody-Rose, 1984– author.
Title: Flung throne / Cody-Rose Clevidence.
Description: Boise, Idaho : Ahsahta Press, 2017. | Series: The new series ;
  #84
Identifiers: LCCN 2017032499| ISBN 9781934103791 (pbk. : alk. paper) | ISBN
  1934103799 (pbk. : alk. paper)
Classification: LCC PS3603.L498 A6 2017 | DDC 811/.6—DC23
LC record available at https://lccn.loc.gov/2017032499

for my dad

"Or I may be a single drop of rain, but I will remain—"

ACKNOWLEDGMENTS

Versions or pieces some of these poems have appeared in *The Denver Quarterly, The Journal Petra, Hold: A Journal, West Branch, Verge, E:Ratio,* and *No Infinite.* Thank you to all those editors. And thank you especially to Sara Nicholson, C. Violet Eaton, Jane Gregory, Elaine Khan, and Nick Gulig for shaping my thoughts and for keeping ideas about poetry in my life. And I am Endlessly Grateful to Janet Holmes and all of Ahsahta Press for consistently putting out such beautiful and interesting books. I'm so honored to be on your press, and to Janet especially for persisting through the chaos of my typesetting without murdering me, and for being Excellent.

CONTENTS

KING//DOM

[st]utter in riddled chain-link [lim]it a body
an unstable [volt]age. dense [mus]cled [s]urge
thru muck dark & primal [b]lushed [bit]ter
mire or [f]lux in form. wing or [gi]zard, stem
in sprout, [sun]lit gimmick [bl]ossom or [g]litter
gash the wet sea open fin or fang pain [p]ried
loose a ridge or [s]pine. tense [mus]ical
[sc]ales condensed syrinx from [sum]mer
[plum]age or graft. limb. teeth or tin, mem-
brane [shel]ter. I wake up in a city. humans
wake up in [ci]ties. in [fl]esh, [f]lash, vast,
[car]ve or [g]naw a niche, [gli]tch my [l]ove-
[s]ong this [ph]ylum in [s]kin or [king]dom in noise.

F̶L̶U̶N̶G̶

" . . . Where all life dies, death lives, and Nature breeds,
Perverse, all monstrous, all prodigious things,
Abominable, unutterable, and worse . . ."

—MILTON, *Paradise Lost*

[AGATE/ALGAE]

mucL:;;::::;;;;:VVV;;;;scscscccc:::;;;;;;;;;;;XS::;;::;;:SCCC;c;c:C:C;c;c:S;::

:::;;;;;;;;;;;;sULC;;;;;||||||;;:;;;;;;;;;;b:b;::bddvdvvdddp|||:::;;;vow||eelLl::;;

;;;;;;vulc;;;;;;;;;;v||\\uil;;;;;>::;;;;;;;;;;;||||||\\::::;|;;;;;||;'\;\;;*||*:;;;;;;::aen:

WWW::;;;;;;;;;;v;;;;;;;;i;;;;;OOO;oo;oOO::;;;P|||xxx\||::;;::;;;prot;aeon:;;;;

oxy::vv::|;::;;;;sulpH;;::;nnyyytgn||;::;;;;;||;;\;\:::vv;;;;;;;;ggg;;;;g;g;;ttLL;

;;;;;gree;;::NNnn::;bluE;;;:thrr:;;:||::;;;;;;Own;;;:o:ochr::;;;eous:;GORG::;

:;;;;|;;|;;;;>;>;H;;;;;;;;;::\|||\neb||::;;;;;;N;;;;;;;hy:;;;dro::ne::;;NEt;;:;vv

;;;;viLe;;;;;||;;;::|||;;;;;agate::;;|\\::;;lgae|:::;;:;||:..:;;>;;...::..;gliLlllILllLLL|

|\||\\VV;;;;;;;;;;b:;;;;zirc:;;::ZZZ::::::V:;;:Z::Z:::ircon::;;V::;;Ony::;x::v:

:::;drab:;;:::::::;;;R::;asp:;;;;er::;;|||\>.v|\\pzzzle:;>;.::::sesire::;;sesss;;::iR::;d

es:;;ir:e::AUR;;;:;;VllZLZL::;;;horz:;;;;;v;:;;N;;N;;hnnHH;;:;;Oxy::g:em

N::;;;iron:;;;brea:;;vv:;;;;;|\\TTthh:;;;;;titan:;|||\s:;ssssV:;;up::;swept::;;blu;

;from::;;;;blue::;;;;green:;;;;||||ll,;;;;;x;;x;z;;;;zzz;;;|\\breath::;;;;;;;;;;;|||\;;;;;|||\

||||::breathe:;;:death:;|::|';:\...;rock::;;s;;;;;s;;;:S:;;s;sss;;;\\\:;;|||sway||:;s;;;;

::::;|\;;|\;;|\\from:;;;;;vioL:;;;;||\viole:;nt::;;oceans::depth:;;;;|\;;;;;\\\:::::vie|

|sac||::|;;;;;||curse|:::d|:::::::;;;;;||xxx|;;\x::;;;;;|:::|::|:;;;;;;vVvVs&tosssed|:;

:;;;;;;;;;;volitile:;;;||;:||::::||||;;;;donned:mantle::::;;;;;;;;;;:\::\:;;>>&sulk::;||||

;;;;uncentered.enclosure;;;;|;:\:|;;rapt:;;;;/pressed::;;;;::>X&;;;x;;::x;;/brok

enopen::\;\vile;;ofblue;;;vial::;of:;;;green:::sea-struck   nerve;;;an   open.;;

;;proto-eye.::;.;;;.opened   in::;an;.::;;ocean;;;;;;;:zZ::;|:|>::|;:::sss::;;:X:;;;

·   ·   ·   ·   ·   ·   ·   ·   ·

· ·   ·   ·   ·   ·   ·   ·   ·

·   ·   ·   · ·   ·   ·   ·

o   i   v   i   s   p   h   x   u

ru   ss   cx   yy   ot   jk   vbb   n

aster   isk   oid   ph   I   yla   sh   ish   gif   arc

dict   tly   ion   ver   mir   glass   nn   ect   ly   s

6

vol   itil   ness   geo   eoa   crut   isl   arch   eon

gutsy   idyl   dol   delphinium   be wracked   by thee

them sudden   them sunlit shores   ripe or be reaped   by thee

sung vulcan cloud built rock by breaking rocks vile earth O
mine algal loudness pressed clean by palm by surge   the rock sky

hung, pony, like the moon, hard up in heaven, then by fire built the sky
lit round the rock-crowned earth that grew an eye to see it

I ache, I arc, I archaic, I arch, I eon, Ion, & on, archembryonic, vie, vision
as minerals ache toward light, as crystals crowd toward heat, as motion

is in me still, stallion of the oceans froth & scum, beat back & forth &
blue & greenblack against the rigid rock-cliffs, the sulphur-spray like
chrysanthemums heaped upon the shore; snot of the oceans; nectar

of the gods. (internal rhyme that first ocula, why wait for language,
proto-eye, protoplasm, protozoic, & yet zoic, why wait for sexual
reproduction, be pre-loined, pre-pulsed, press gems thru a thin
membrane, thief, pervert, from the first—)

clean my carbon flute of being. polish the first tarnish off. sway, sea-lily,
sea-bitten areole of living. thou parasite. thou spineless, sapless dove-
cell, I owe you, ok, pre-ganglia, pre-biont, accident, ignoble of form
& yet noble, philic & urgent my pathetic, my shining ancestor of form.

storm-ridden pleiad. ochre-in-the-hands. chronos, chronomic, & yet
nomic. cyanoaccretion, capsized heart on the pre-flowers of the first
morning, slimed & ugly pre-orchid. pre-euclid & insignificant cyto-
plasm that heaves & subsides as a film on the ocean, silver then blue.

curse, gentle primordial clouds, rain down a dull mist to sweep the
leaden sea, the rusting sea, precipitating order from urge, accreting order
inside urge, illium, cerulean, cut back from pride, methane, dust, solar
flare, from sea to shining, foul odor, curse of the open eye, curse of the
formless made form, the sea looked back at you then & then grew
clouded, lidded, heavy with the weight of sky, sullen w the weight of sky.

a darkness shines in the darkness timid as an eyeball, sightless as a rock.
a darkness shines in the darkness a cloud covers the sun the shadow of a
thought, shadow of a face turning away, a dimness shines around & is
swallowed, a small gulp, catch-in-the-throat, a brief disturbance in the
pattern; it was no rock that opened itself into itself onto that rock throne.

do all minerals strain toward living? porous silicates, clay, pyrite, both
code & catalyst, the silver spray catches in the light, would it have
caught in the darkness also, made an inside out of it, an instant out of it,
the ragged shore is wide & bright with the patterns etched in rock.

"my heaven is brass & iron my earth" & to be the body torn nevertheless
in the fields of copper, to invent exile, "shed thy grace [on]"—& to be the
unclad bodies of first discipline inside all the extremities of the earth.

tempest-tossed, mineral cluster, mined from the lava that runs as rivers
of rock, be still my, be strewn my, flowers of hydrogen, drenched

in the endless chemistry of light. Proteus, becalmed, be calm, the sea.

8

*

speak, rock. like a bad tongue, ugly in the mouth of the world.

speak, first nerve, first chord, now-cold sea
seed in lace blooms by the grey shore first sign.

hard rocks horde crystals under oceans, speak, nitrogen
    speak, carbon, reek genesis like the first breath.

    acidic ocean of forgetting, second sign
            is quartzite, pink like an eye
            upturned in the metamorphic face

                who ate hir children as rocks
        speak, children of rocks
                    radiated, ultra-violet, sinuous Lethe

    who ate first rocks radiant in the night-sky,
                grew slowly.

*

who called out into that other colored sky
who hatched the sky, hatched into it, parasitic
from dew made be by godless gas sullen
unangel'd garden ringed round by a thin
fatty membrane
　　in the sulphur diaphanous

*

　　　　　　　　speak, face,
　　　　pre-Nectarian, moonless, brute,
　　　　blind sky what
　　　　　　　　ashen rain falls
　　　　as sparks.

cyst
cryst
al

distal
Dis
Troy

try
umph
!

morph.
I
(s)ing

finch,
finch!
ox.ide.

cad
mium,
u.

~~god~~
~~god~~
etc.

beryl
illium
x

an-
oxic
dox

para
tetra
dactyl

sph
Eye
rynes

night
roGen
isis

nuc
leo
tidal

gal
ax.
y.

gar
b
led

rib
o!
some,

am
in
O

look,
a
minnow!

pre
se
X, m.

&
y
not

new
fang
-led

char
ybd
Is

lux
et
lux j/k

Veritas
my
@ss

CYAN.O.RADI.ANC.IC.HYD.RA.IDE.
SOL.ARW.IND.DRIV.EN.NEBULA.RIZ
ING.PAR.DOX.ASTER.OID.BRILI.ANC
.RAIN.BR.ILLIANT.MIST.CARB.ON.ZIRC
.IC.METHYL.FAINT.YOUNG.SUN

URGE ORDER ACCRETE
AMASS EGREGIOUS GORGEOUS
solvent "falls out of solution"

SHED [THY] "GRACE" │ HADES
    a draped mantle
o'er the bare shoulder'd earth

                the risk of asteroids is very great
                the sun is very faint

        the sum
    cumulus
        of all things
            is rock,
    vapor
        & light

                .

            &
            a light
        rain falls often

                .

12

until the sky is a sky
& underneath the sky
the ocean is an eye that blinks
as a wind sweeps across it
hush of the first ocean
each ion a need, each cling 2 each
form crystals, grow crustal & bold

    we are late for the bombardment
    the heavens rain down bright rocks
    the surface winces & turns over
    like a dreaming giant

[REFT MOON A SOCKET & DUST THERE]

        around its own
            fire, atoms
             of my atoms,
         pale yellow
            bloom forms
        around hir eyes

   .

      the pale
      sea
    gathers itself
  in the pale sun

VULCAN   VIRIDIAN
JOULES HEAPED UPON JOULES

thou banquet
unquiet [] formless
bouquet

dreary of rock
　::seek //

　　.

a pattern climaxes at a form
a living form is restless within itself
a light rain, a dense fog, minerals dissolved
in the clear heavy air precipitate, rain down
veins like veins of ore calcify,
oxidize, catalyze, cringe

　blink in the salt anoxic
　hyperbolic
　& stung—

***

OROGENIES laconic timidity
buzzard SIRE in my essence
-ozoic bilateral eternal neptune
pulse VIEW & eroded to valley

STITCH reft welt seam spire SWIFT
give back SHY now crystalline
now ash now watch now ask
"no one has ever seen a granite
batholith intrude"

GIVE ME rupt struct candidly
"the symphony of the earth" avail
clumsily it MIRROR there ish
ithic SILT tilt back ATLAS at last

stratigraphy sphere pear(il) purse
HEAVE heaven HEAVE ocean
yr answer is wrong seek

[meteorite.moonlight.MILKY THE WAY
& MILKY THE DEEP.biota.the[atmo]
sp/heres.plummet&hurl.hurt/le.thru.vast.is
a dim.radio.metabolizing.the.light

cyclops w fistfulls
of lashes bent
violets burnt
off'rings blue
ashes blue
as hir
veins blue
as hir
eye.

shake // loose
yr golden

wounded

shake // loose
yr golden
goose
down
titan, let
down your golden
tear.

xe, giant.
be muscled in dew,
vengeful & angry
in the soft mist cling
only 2 thunder,
only 2 rocks.

thy shrine
is the trampling
of violets

u whose fist
crumbles rocks
be soft,
be soft,

who in fitful
& dreaming
clenches the one eye
to the heavens
the one fist
full of snow.

***

ish be ick prick b gaunt zem "said" then
absence in virtu en situ heart-hurt ich is ness
be dire dove & cold yet YE DUMB BEASTS
come forth

eon arginine adamant twined lover
silly in the being of it full up & sick

palmate, abscess, herald of whatever
in ingot, got god good, beat him then, u shh
of a prion, pervert, a mirror is "grappled" o o o "lay him down"
& guzzlt then thh ill't lic't by me make naked of. oh
sodden? then hurt then! anathema ye swarm
yet swam then—

:

.

u have come forth
in the half-light

into the sea

cut into the meadow
roiling w dusk

glaciation, cuss,
u stand, as a man (ish)

in the open

dumb as the dumbest beast
that dumbly beats the earth

***

MINE EYES MINE MINES MINE DIAMONDS MINE DIADEM CREPT
AS DAWN CREPT THEN, CREATURAL ON THE HILLS A CORONET
MINE THE DEEP SHAFT & FALLING MINE THE DARK PLUMAGE THE
ENDLESS PITCH THROUGH AIR MINE DAZZLE MINE MUZZLE MINE
SIGNET MINE IS A RINGING IN AIR, AMETHYST, OZONE, FIRST SIGN
FIRST PRISM IS THE DEED OF LIGHT & STRANDED THERE, HAZARD
OF LIGHT, BLUE AS A CYCLOPS EYE SET IN THE COLD BROW OF
THE SEA, THE METALLIC & URGENT MOUTH OF THE SEA GROWS
ELECTRIC IN THE SUNS INCESSANT RAYS & INCITES A CHAIN
REACTION INTO ALL THE THINGS.

***

perspire, there, trumpet-lily, throat
of the ocean, the shore
littered w fragments,
the shore
made of new rocks
fresh heaved
& untouched
that crash
& crush
& grind
on each other
with a new frenzy
a new shine
a keen glint
in the eyes
of the rocks

mica-white
rock-roses
bloom then
on the cliffs
overlooking the sea

***

citrine & milky & rose, jasper, feldspar, lapis & flint, tigers-eye,
olivine & smoky, calcite & tourmaline, onyx, beryllium, emerald,
chalcedony & chert. slate slate slate salt ruby gold lead dead sea.

[what gaze were the colors for, then, what plumage,
display, nemesis of sight—or was it a joy]

***

Aster[isk] pull // pooled forth
a firm[amen]t A metal Gate
cloud from mount borne bare

& blasted, craterous, spent.

Beggar, stampede, ice, stampede,
nature u vice, u clamber'd horizon,
u breach & u break & u curse

@ the sudden & piercing of light.

& the swelling & pouring of light
particulate. agony, dire
profusion multiplied by light

by force all maimed, plucked earth.

Some gnarly Dignity spread
eagle on the soft rocks, spring,
after a hard frost, u, there

come suddenly forth.

into the barren, the being of
being on this Particular earth.

minotaur nemean lion sphinx etx
rhino megatherium possum
poodle ephesus pegasus
polyphemous who were those
women raped by the centaurs
pterodactyl microsporidium heron

cassiopoea medusa the erinyes
armadillo charybdis tantalus chrome
the chariot that brought demeter under
each cell in its cage

allele aeon eros & argos
hunter & gather yr bow strings r taut

vanquist squisht squander squat

blades
~~leaves~~ of grass

       perplext

then there was a long period of silence

OPULENT & PLENTIFUL GLOBS MADE BODIES MADE SILT LIVED
IN IT BY THE SEA SHORE FOAM MADE BUBBLES SLIME MADE
MOLD MADE PLASM MADE MORE OF IT MADE GLYCOGEN &
CARBOHYDRATES AMINO ACIDS PROTEINS INVENTED GREEN ATE
IRON ATE NITROGEN PUSHED PROTONS THROUGH A MEMBEANE
BECAME ELECTRIC THEN THE OXYGEN SWELLED THE SWELTERING
THE GOD DAMN OCEAN FULL OF THINGS PROTISTS RADIOLARIA
DIATOMS MADE MORE GREEN SO MUCH GREEN & OTHER GREENS
"CERULEAN" & "PUCE" MADE POLYPS CALCIFIED MADE SHINY SILICA
SPIRES OF THEMSELVES & BARB'D & PEARL'D EATEN ATE SUN ATE
EACH OTHER BURPED OUT AN ATMOSPHERE SWARMED IN VAST &
SOGGY COLONIES FLOATED BELLY UP OR UPSIDE DOWN TENTACLED
POISONOUS MADE CORAL LACE MADE FANS NETS CAUGHT & GOT
CAUGHT GOT STUCK GOT SYMBIOTIC ENDOSYMBIOTIC PARASITIC
OR JUST EATEN INTO ELECTRONS & SUGARS & GAS MADE MATS
STAYED WET ON SAND MADE DIRT BY DYING BY EATING DEATH
& DYING THEN BY FERMENTING THE DEAD & SHINY BODIES INTO
AIR MADE SHELLS MADE ENEMIES MADE PALACES OF THEMSELVES
MADE TOWERS TO LIVE IN MADE OF THEIR BODIES RADIAL DIALS
MADE OF THEIR BODIES PRISMS & TUBES MADE OF THEIR BODIES
WHIPS & PROPELLERS GLOSSY ARTIFACTS LAID DOWN IN THE
PRIMORDIAL STRATA THEY MADE I GUESS THE WHOLE WORLD
FROZE OVER THEN & THEY HID IN THE HOT CRACKS & CREVASSES
OF THE EARTH RUBBING THEIR SOFT MUCUS ON EACH OTHER TO
EAT EACH OTHER WRAPPING THEIR PHAGOCYTE ARMS AROUND
EACH OTHER MADE INTERNAL ARCHITECTURE DOUBLED THEM-
SELVES & TRIPLED THEMSELVES BY SOME FREAK DUPLICATION &
TRIPLICATION & METAMORPHOSIS & MASS KILLING BY HEAT BY COLD
BY OXYGEN BY NITROGEN BY FALLING ROCKS BY DISSOLVED IRON BY
THERE NOT BEING ENOUGH OF EACH OTHER TO EAT BY THERE NOT
BEING ENOUGH SUNLIGHT TO EAT BY THERE BEING TOO MANY
OF THEM THEY CROWDED EACH OTHER OUT OF THE SUNLIGHT
OUT OF THE HEAT THEY DRIED OUT IN THE AIR THEY EXCRETED
SLIME ON THEMSELVES MADE PLUMES & WRIGGLED & FLOWED
SOFT AS WALKING FEATHERS FLOATED AS INCANDESCENT BAGS

GREW PHOTOSENSITIVE PLASMA GREW FRONTAL & MOTIVE MADE
ELECTRIC BY SUGAR MADE NERVE TWITCH NERVE FORWARD
SENSING THE SEAS THE TIDES THE RAINS THE DAYS THE NIGHTS
THE DEATHS & FUMES & DEPTHS WERE WASHED ASHORE & MADE
NEW BY THE SHORE BY THE DEPTHS BY THE RAINS BY THE TIDES BY
THE LIGHT & BY THE ATMOSPHERES THEY MADE & THEY WERE PINK
WITH THEIR FEATHERS CNIDARIANS THEY GLOWED IN THE NIGHT
THEY BURROWED INTO THE SLIME OF THEIR ANCESTORS MADE
OF THEMSELVES A SEMBLANCE OF SYMMETRY OF THEMSELVES &
ARMORED IT IN PLATES & THORNS & SPINES & CLASHED IN THE DEPTHS
& RAMMED EACH OTHER ON THE SHORES & BORED HOLES THROUGH
EACH OTHER & TURNED TOOTHY AND BOLD & GREW HUGE AND
NUMEROUS IN THE LIGHT & IN THE DARKNESS BEHIND THE LIGHT
& MADE OF THEMSELVES MORE FRUITFUL & MULTIPLE MADE MORE
BIZARRE FORMS TO CROWD OVER THE IMMENSE & ANIMATE EARTH.

Imbecile, acquire noise in inmost region, psalm & flood-plain replication

speak again, bastard, garble it, first throat, choked first. how long a
hollow is anchored, breeds open, raptor, captor, larva, shell & home

come sudden, starlings, of the monstrous egrets, scaled, taloned, vines hung
w fat flowers, vascular plants perspiring, of the edges of things touching all
the other things in the heat & of the claw marks & of the teeth

& the thirst of forests, the living thirst of each tree, each night is a forest,
I am dendritic & lonely, a swarm, there is a thing it is shining, there is a
thing it is shining in, in the field of all the things, spinning; some ferns.

dare it to speak in its excess. dare the momentary out of it, passionless
flower u close like an eye in darkness. u close like a mouth in darkness.
you are no angel postulating yrself over the bare surface of everything.
you are no angel in either the darkness or the light you eat like an ugly god

the dead slime bodies of light. corrode me there in excess by oxygen,
heat, by need, eat, mold of the first furl pressed flat into mud, spore, germ,
preliminary gut, foothold, resin, niche, the long low moan of rivers
shifting as veins across the surface, cutting through the first face; regard
me, face, under the harsh light & circling wind, circle, wind, turn.

& turning, turn into, mutant-child of the first fern, first fish, lisping
thru mud u ugly ugly pulse, eroded, honed, plated & horned,
cloud-dim & saural lizard-eye, prance, cold cathedral, fuck the
young sun in its singing there erects a stasis of noise in that first
night "I'm here" "I'm here" they say, pink is my new color, pollen,
proboscii & odor. unhumble me to enter that cathedral where I am,
already "more suave, more goofy than" form, u runt

of color, claim inherent in the field where there is a fold grow a
small hoof, eye, small tooth, divide, meotic sea, salty & electric
w rare gracelessness, grow gleeful, freakish, hunted, vicious w
need & desire, abscond w more pulp dormant in seed, loom of the
frightful oceans heave, weaving, wave back, clematis.

come sudden, hopscotched horizon in the morning, finch, battle, razor-
wing, see to it that the world is carved, be made then by eye, by wing,
by habitat & echo, huddle me, puddle, from sun made meat a body of,
come sudden, green w living, bruised in the early skin, violets clenched

as offerings in the fisted cyclops, he cries with his one eye, calm
me, city, coral, curse. be driven from form to form, thirst to thirst,
under the new sky come stumbling, come suddenly, things,

script, data, helix, chloroplast yearn 4 sun urge the small cells up, sac
& "glisten" sac: listen, a field upon which a pattern reacts in the ocean,
radiate, fold upon, cloudy the surface milky & churning then spin then.

move ye silent in the pride beheld, ingrate of amphibian & bitch,
song strung taut over the surface of the world, inheld, be jewel
(be cruel) my blue green world. be gross w life, be gross w me

plume, hollow fur, falter, blush, dumb roar, dull pain, unfurl—
mammalian sadness, dim of the open, flecks in the dull eye, swoon

for a bright & a bitter sun then make ache of the granite, sugars

crave structure, make fat crystals in sunlight, make meat make noise

IN FORM LEFT
MARKS U

UNANGELIC

SNAIL SLUG CHOIR
OF SELF-PROPULSION.

THE DAY SUFFERS ITS SUNSET / NO IT DOESN'T / AND THIS IS TRUE
NO IT'S NOT / ANTHROPOMORPHIX SH*T / DO YOU / AREN'T I
METAMORPHIC/ SHIST / CAMBRIAN / CAN I BE / ABLE
DEW DOESN'T / SWEAT IS / MOUNTAINOUS / SUDDEN / IT IS SO
INSIGNIFICANT / HOW 2 WITHSTAND / THE DAY / THUS / LOOM

IDLE DIES DEEP SOME SUMMER SINGS SLOW ME A GREAT
PASTURE / ALL RISE / WEPT / CARBON / CARBON / CLAIM
IS THIS TRUE? / FAULT LIES / DEEP / IN THE EARTH

pilfer]lichen
appetite

      jealous the fortress
      wireless]night

yolk]matter
heed // hedon
nist—halt, dew

      track matter
      ]mud, come

empty of all eyes

lisp, cusp, sip, dare
drink, soak, apt, snare

      ]dwell]tantrum
      rank city
      Odysseus
f   orth—

ugh astonisht
cup lip some sun

      ]crept

matter-of-fact
]point taken, bough
2 neck—

      &
      scarce]
      provided—

this makes a break & fills it. a glass
floats on a pond. a disc dissolves
the horizon of an eye, gloss
& slick of it. encompass.

diffract each shaft
in lash & tide

& close the open

& lie upon it.

*

this makes a break & fills it. no garden
guards me. the perimeter is pierced.

this breaks me & then fills me,
shy & violent as it is.

*

synchronous] aspire
"a spire"— lost //

SYNCH sunk | drunk
] swallow god //

behold: ew] shucked
shell—weird costume

cloud] CAUGHT get
got] hymn then clawed //

flawed rock | "adrift"
a gift—plucked

RIM or reason] totally
fucked—rivers, revolt!

zoom in] kiss this
—VOLUMINOUS //

wish]—spent—
]'s, "pent" nest //

SOUGHT rest | last
rite] spheric —become //

be: cause] vital
ounce—UNGUENT

MUSCLE—cost
] most must 'scape //

36

"from whence" | vital
]flock—grasp //

synch | STOP—

(eye) glaciate (green) (undergrowth)
like (lichen) (prism) O2 (vascular)
metabolic (fancy) sugar // sugar

wept (circle) succumb.

hex-bolt (cylinder) cut (hydrogen) (horizon)
in glass (mark radial) mine (mine)
taste (bud) alluvial (socket)

cartilage cartilage bone.

pursue (gallant) (grace) ice (angle)
geode-form (swallow me) time-lapse
unstable isotope (hyacinthine) (boom)

I have seen the regret in the eye of the seasons.

(phylum) cull ("grace") (extinction)
redox electric (flare) (grow cryst)
in lung (astonisht) seize (up)

haploid (hapless) desire (a body)

stone (stone) crude (sap:oil) regret
hazard // allegory (glint) (fracture)
ape (abyss) know this

& this & this.

i i ii iii i i x i x i i ix x c c i xx c c i i i i x x e
e ei ei ai x v vi vie x x is s xi si sx iie lie ll lix xii xii
cill lixx c cc ciii cll zll z z z z z z z i zi zii ziie ziel lize zli air
xxx cc z z xiix ziiizll z lilis slil slii eyssill sllixx xxccci cciiill clslll
zlzle slslsei zzz i i i sllsi iisll eiix aaiill lillz lilliz lilliez illez illeze
zelllillzzxx xllxle xllcy ccyll clyllz zleill vvv vlil vvill villlelei isllaz
zliilelw ww www wliii lllo o oolll iiool ooiiilzz zzoozle ooze
sloooz zlooozle cllleezyyl cllleyr riclll ccrrrillll crillllrilll cerulean
uuuu ullean nnlleall meleell meillliz mzzzle ooozlm soon zoon
zonal sxnlllz znallx xnnally xnay snzl znllaull verrrllzllz zlrrl! rrrr
syntxxxxiic ccillic icillic xxillm xylem cerebellum swoonnzzzili
swrrlli ccoccous crocus ccrestetted tterxx circxz rxxrll axxim mnxxx
snllle yllrl yrllw rly? rllyicx vvvlli vvice cice eyessziz sizh slllzz
zznallic   mtlallix xxeptoptrycx xpt pszzzlt ccrownt ccrise z x
pppppppppph pppsh lllvt vvlletic epileppxic ccloudttburrzts vieey
ffffff fxxr ouxghttxyt lllslxlz zisle isle shy isle eye slighteyeisle might
vvverstt immerzzt islple izls mnx scrr flew flutexsnare flllxkrscarez
ixmyselfvserc scrimzx szx trumpet sayzitriumphant iz is lilxis
elixroflove islilysosweet isicczl sllezlyish isp aspicc isheartsixk
zontidont   abysmmaliztheblink   brinkiihaveaheavyhteight
isaneyebrightisslthishallelujiaishismmyaglanceisatwarxxxhaltisthismy
basilisk ish izish izzat dear2 u o && volatile is the daffodil oozing dew

grime diadem my mock-frog-heart & pulse & belch thy croak thy peeping crocus in the catechism of mud u r the fingered data of the urge u r the heartthrob in the photovoltaic field, u plow thru the night-sky, wide, arc, disturb the ripple in me, bog in there, & shine, where there is a rift in it, be filled each crack in us, I have dapper & condemned myself, mud thy crown thine silk thy spine u urchin of godhead u sucker of dew U THROB IN THE MOONLIGHT U LEGION OF FROGS U DEAD & UNNUMBERED & UNNAMED U DAMNED & DISASTROUS OF BODIES U SWOON u spring forth from the muck of the bog in the shine of the stars & the wind in wild fury & the wind in sweet nectar & the wind in the rampant & cyclic decay of the seasons, u r the eye of the Cyclops u r the plural & groaning, there is no mercy deep in the lizard don't make me say mercy deep in the lizard

THERE HAS BEEN A GREAT MISTAKE.

glow, grow bright internal, internet, nuptial fling into dark waters,

come electric as a sudden eye turning on, blink, the salt that
stung stings now corrosive on the filaments, labyrinth of spiders,

take this telescope, now "rare earth"—tantalum capacitor—

my radio—out of the static rises static I point my mineral eye
towards an outward telescope of snow, the static pours from

the stars, circles us, the static streams out our bodies

& all the other bodies particulate, superconducting a relentless
pulse, my nanotech eyeball constricts in the sudden light, spin,
pain is a needle of noise arcing across the synaptic globe, glow,

digitalsun digitalstarling micron-ellipse, cliff-hung haploid
& singing, data of the echo, tidal rhyme condenses to an order,

heaving signifier of the place marked by urge, be bright, be
solemn in yr choosing, words are ends, end sudden, come
into the network, path marked by mucosa, throbbing, sight

with stillness caught & ringing there the wide blue gaze of sky
comes flooding in, what doesn't break englobes us, pantheon of
my manhood, of the electromagnetic vines wreathed upon the
world, the earth is heavy,heaving, microbial & teething, atom-

of-my-atom, diadem, how do you comprehend, erasure of all
cities, blink, limbic thrust in the namesake of the day, order is
a myth of patterns made by living, rising syllabic, say I am no

more a man, meshwork of sun on waves, apex of a form come
wordless, the shining encircles us, net of lace in which the eye

that I am is caught in the world, telescopic, escape me, hunted thing, titanium & scrap, there is no silence there is glitter on the surface & glitter in the eyes & glitter in each electric thing that sings itself to sleep galactic in the spinning field, aster, mastering me, trumpet-flower

ask me, statistically speaking, eclipse of the oceans eye, my money is on the universe, strike me down w an answer, a silent aura crowns the northern horizon, unbent & axial glance, stratospheric lithography, chart this arc of territory, I am able, u are a pulse of quartzite away, hold yr ear to the ground, u can hear the tires on the highway offset the earths spin;

each creature that crawleth, remote-controlled, drone in a magellenic wind, upon the viscid surface, face me, momentous of electron, dare me to stare down the sun, the sun wins, can u believe it, this howling ache of a prism in us, the mountains thrust up, pull apart, fill in the outwash plains w sediment & cracks w molten ore, oceans dry to salt, accumulate elsewhere, form glaciers, cut canyons in us, sift thru us

for crystals in us, there are no angels, zygote of a globe careless in its rhyming & careless in its urging forth, please be yielding, supple as ripe fruit, grim elapse, harmony in the dim pursuit of seasons, eons, my nemesis, the sky, so much of it, circling, be the vulture of my eye in excess, the earth's crust rises tidal to the dumb moon, thumb-in-the-eye

of the dumb moon, soar, satellites, on wings of solar-cells, blink into the dark night "I'm here" "I'm here"—shutter, click, boom, come into the excess, I place a GPS upon a hill, lol, u are my anthem, myth of the wilderness, make it stop, make it stop spinning, sightless glucocorticoid receptor in the interstice, spermatozoa blooming at an

ungodly rate, algae, choke the sea thy mother, swim in me, phthalates, bisphenol, polyascetalyne, all nets cast come up empty, sworn enemy of the loom, if the eye is a net let it come up empty, silver-gold, blue-green, crash course in molecular physics, streaming data from a million million sources into the calyx, photobiont, severed nerve severed first

into orbit   then lay down in the passive matrix   in the digital stream
name all the creatures anew   organic light-emitting diodes
in the forest   ephemeral   in the endless plasma   I told u
2 lay down   w yr golden polymer   w yr robes of interstitial dew

w yr robotic lens   sailing outward   in the ringing symbiology of

noise   take this fragment   animal of utter instinct   of utterance

formed parasitic   of sun   paradisic   surging   data of the urge

not all desire is climactic   forest of the iris   stitched 2 the world

hermaphrodidic   antennae, sing to me   moss

neo-lithic   archangel   mistake   of the

reckless   urge   seething   ironic

myth   ic   isotope   of the noble   unmade

sun   unelectric   heir   —

from SCUM, REJOICE

[<>
{INDWELLING}

sun = ~~god~~: human habitat

umwelt what is given *taken* {made}
　　[is able] : [grasped]

abject, senseless self-organization

"MEMBERS OF BRUTE ~~CREATION~~"

sun son g utter "autopoesis" [is]
"~~self-contained~~" SELF = SEA

[be meadow be prairie be city, beast
be] only Only

　　　　　　　　　　　　]

// <>

membraned pond-silt o we are wept
the dimness in us. what is most raw
flabbergasted joy that we are

<>

feast on meadow, lack. warm-blooded blue-hearted intent latent in us
how ripped open prairie that we are squeamish how stunned

o eukaryotic lust! cut-throat down to white pith the ugly song
how stunted the sun over the meadow how stung—

glut in what rapt
pandemonium

what wet sinew   wire

          strewn

<>

rhyme me parched diction
delicate truce. rhyme me
liar, plucked where lay
what captured

     majesty

adorn

<>

.

crust :: nectar :: diodes
  blush :: glutton :: leap

o Andromeda yr asterix a fool

                    [
         x get all salty & slip-shod this
                   stunt of spring a cheating
         heart-sick
            apparatus of field

       lust & vault of star-spangled
                basal ganglia & "song"]

.

bright pond to wine,
water, to wind, wound
bright wound, to open

<>

bright pond to wine,
water, to wind, wound
bright wound, to open—

open wound to thrust out
what light, which meadow

eviscerating grace there we
Capture | Impart

[stalk grace // by which
we touch // that there is
implicit Territory—]

[terror or error]

recoil, seed, Surrender
sling me Human into
Vegetal no hum dry combat

what do u know, system, noise of what
Voltage, winged Radii, Consume.

green field,T
Meadow=Machine
of Meadow

rend us
tear us

from where we first   .]

<>

this slang bestiary—summer's Flute
what limb or limbic I

 stalk
"tooth & nail"

dragonless the post-traumatic wild.

untame ≠ garden.
claw = law. [vanquish]

& what wilderness
succumbs, graceless
forms defy.

[loot what plenty—
grace I rip—]

this illegal territory twists & rose
to hazard, the edge of lux.
(us|ury) "o lay me down"

"on the lam(b)"
or, famine.

\<\>

[having made out like a bandit
I blame what gilt blooms on
suffer, cadmium, lace.

grandiose the raving clouds
the salvaged mud I eat
& sing no song just grunt
& trash-talk, heckle
starlings & that one stupid
animal I, fleshless, crave]

<>

bloom a
forest

larynx tuber
slip marsh-

dark what
have u swallow

-ed heave up
a valley sm-

all flower u
choked sprout

greedy u
viscera to tulip

-bulb thick
w greed

& w caress

<>

[ok so tell me what is most real
how we have to kill to eat

space we brutal, claim, o be
gentle o be joyful
in the mirror

of the field eye-
axis in blue sky-
fold red in the throat
thru a hole in it singing

o & o & oh forever]

. . . . .
. . . . .

pardon this
barbaric episode

<>

sleaze embryonic scales
ectoplasmic gears rattle
in the throat of the throat
of the organism

"shake, rattle & roll" Rock
my currency I garble & own
a tongue a trigger a raw

hide. idol dior oil a lush murk
a prey down to slay a prayer
to slake some thirst on muck

& carrion this carnal
knowledge this prefrontal
inhibition

& ruffle, also, & pluck & puke
& croon elegant in feral etc,
you know.

\<\>

EDENTATA

OPUS

nestled the valley // nuzzlt it

dare me to enter what is already open.

dare to bar the boughs to the meadow. some are alive.
they are green w it & thirsty.

get inside the software of the meadow
hack & flee w it. then

suckle the damsel &
bar the boughs before me.

MIRE EYES

FOLD THEN

thrusting

mynx-hybrid
nano-digitalis

the world is what makes us

animal
holds us ~~down~~ up

.

heliopteryx abysmal gonad
surround a man

w
coward
/
w
embrace

.

form perform function

free me from

a body is

not enough.

PRY ME
PLY ME

from where we first—]

<>

—Mace me bright atlas
where there is surrender—

[sunder & render]

—or, where there is, Surrender—

Rampant Viral Rapture Dumb With Light
Dig In The Rot Earth It's Rot Still, Thick
Caress. Deficient Mitosis Of Nothing
No Thing. Wind, Endless Desire For Wind,
Open, Re-converging Nonsensical
Want Shakes Us Loose Loses Us

Regardless. Degraded Rupture In What
Plasma. Shatter This Double Vision &
Damn Me Where There Is—

<>

& then u creatures
of the ~~trees~~
          valley u

peel the throat
from the throat
learn skin from kin

heal my triumphant
lily I've cut | yr tongue
this embryonic swamp-
rot loved out loud
   in error
& forgiven there
where we grinning
          sing—

{SYMPHONY}

bell-collision
orchid/ orchestra
strum a stem
to chordata
raw data
in error

crimson
in chrom-
osomal din
drought of
rough ter-
rain

rose/ erosion
preemptive sun-
blast in gut-
ter. inert
terror
my

civil-
ization
still intact
slum and habit
down to gem-
stoned body

in the hum/ an
ordinary slaughter

<<>>

light endures. light endurance
stops a stutter. all this star-

charged brittle stuff
breaks into atomic

ash after. scratch
in lilac or a drain-convoluted dawn

in carcass-strewn. no awe
no awful order. tendril/ shoot-green pistil

lashed to static. acidic river
"out of eden." all this latent

in limb. care-paradox
no perfect form in flesh or leaf

or flash, hit electric. rimmed up/ struck
in glare, no rare, grace

gagged-light all this
ragged flaw in periodic

structure: hydrogen/ breath/ helium
bomb/ swarm, warmer now

dumb dispassionate sun-
light toward which we turn—

grazed periphery . epithet. cut
through the endless wires below the city. where the empty wind-core
hardens & thrusts up is where. schema that depicts the migration
pattern of red clover, cultures of manners, larkspur, plastics, currency,
gestures, terror. schema that traces trace amounts of lead in the water,
sulphur, pollen, blood from somewhere, security cameras, slang;
schema that swings with the rotation of the earth, delirious with
motion & stasis, motion & barriers, floodlights, militia, grammar,
kinds of flowers. schema that swells & cauterizes, finds no fault. faults
an error. arrives again at itself my endless spectrum inward gaze.

+++

let x stand for civilization,
as in xylophone and xenon; let y be distance: yet, yes, yellow; let lust
be time and crumble cities, let a mirror mimic sensation, there are eyes;
f is wind, e is my carbon harvest, my glutton & pride; multiply by 10;
let c stand for laughter; there is a sun in the middle of an iris; let I stand
for singularity; there is a point of infinite density lodged in the gullet,
the opposite of 'to shine' is precision; let b be balance and the silence
after the alphabet. let x mark diamonds and the many eyes of the dead.

+++

blinded "by the light" from which
a million photons blaze abrupt in face-shock; round about as ringed
means "surrounded" where a city edged craze hushes its own hush is
where we laid it down & laid down beside it; stamina is only one kind
of virtue; the flushed raw weeds & skin swell into sunlight; warm-
blooded we flinch & squint; "avert your eyes" yes in hunger or rabid
fury in ultraviolet seeds whereby I cringe a yellow gaze & pass over.
whereby one closes & then another closes.

.

I HAVE FOUND U THERE, first flower, lonely on a rock reaching up
sun was my gait then, & crime my being & u were a word unspoken
in the dire light I stumbled into, slowly, as a hunted thing.

the universe was too big a thing, impossible to hold
on ones spine, petal or stalk. I am weak in my desires, I speak
only to break the silence from the day. what is hidden

is not a treasure, it has not been sought out in the darkness,
it has not been kept.

THRONE

TO MAKE A CROWN OUT OF THE WORLD

// A MEMBRANE OF THE REAL

camouflage ze Chronos eat
by-the-sea-shore, all day
rock-of-my-rock flash
me yr barren boulders suckle
be in a position 2 suckle
the daybreak out of it

by scrotum eyed sun Olympus
in exegesis "many geese"
my chariot my Ford Excursion
Oiled the sun there Oiled it good
& greasy, there

mir mirror miro make muck mirror
make mirror make murk
as mirror is an eye
is an eyes

& eyes will guide eyeward
stammering, half-hurt, half-prey,
Actaeon, see the self is selved
is fragment, mirror, flect
each pain is an ocean each eye
opens each eye up

replication was
my plumage then
a million eyes & stone

A THRONE IS A THROAT UPON WHICH A STONE.

AN IRIS GUARDS THE GATES.

WHAT ONCE WAS BREATHED IS BREATHED BACK.

WHAT ONCE WAS EATEN, ATE.

thrung u tyrant flycatcher my ♥ delinquent
forest upheld, throne crown crow black beak bark
black beak bleak heart bleat or bark in the darkness, meager
little lamb of ivy, wrought & falter
sap the spring does rise bold
in these (our) imaginary bodies & strut
seamless in throng ugly & thorough

& thru & through
u throat & song

moral parallelogram fear me
fear not, iron, nodding bobbin,
leave us, @ best leave me
incomplete

wrap the rock in gauze then swallow it.

. . .

meadow, operationally ransomed tunnel thru dense
foliage concrete & marble there muttering unbeacon
unnimble hoof-print paw me & stumble (I) lonesome
katydid stutter drag "mozart" towards volatile, flora
stole from a nomenclature a name

all names r the same

"apple" "bomb" "lizard" "sine"
 dead thing, turn now, grain-siloh
 subterfuge, forget-me-not, angle-only
 abashed, shame of the first eye (star)
 & spectra, taste, grace
-leaf, climb

a steep path slowly

. . .

mimic a tuneless prometheus then
placeholder in a name, denizen
where a place was held, spit
split lip a stone swallowed then
mutinous & cold

etched appetites strung pearls on thick boughs
where we thought we needed them most;
bought come early, before the shine wears off

in this dalliance the days crust rose gentle
sight : listen, insects, night crows the break awake
grim of salivation, sir I'm resolute,
forsaken, crested, there
in plumage, lorn—

plus per lesion lance man-breast then own
song-stutterer thou regret of nature flung
far from these shores rotten "2 the core"
txt of my slang heart, math of a measured world
whatever each extinction this

marks & "maketh pure"

. . .

I eye in it in instant
grown a gown of slime

undress before the throne.

...

eyeball perimeter lush allegory
replace the need—the need is a place
it is lost in. I am lost
in a place there's a need in.
shuttle, loom, ambient pressure,
girdle the bark, stung nest
unprayer & gentle the bloom.

derive me from no math but this:
alksjdfh lkjsdlfkj lkd glaksjdf askj

& shed thy grace on meeeeeeeeeeeeee

APE|ANGEL

=

u wounded ape have fell
from ~~grace~~ some trees

// big brained &
endless Capacity for
grief—

//

deep in the DNA of a leopard
of a lizard, sphinx, each bird,
crowned Prince, eliminate—
make of it an angel—muscular—ripped—

not to worship

obscenity—

Detonate.

//

u who swallowed cold air in yr fall
split yr tulip-brain inward—u who
r a deep mistake   in the lineage
in the biosphere of yr origin—
a limbic fluke, a force-field upon which
EVERYTHING—brambles in yr brain why
is this happening

??

//

code this crease in me—glory—be—
as perilous—strike—fear—
"into-the-heart" // abstract relation of
& vulgar // touch // crude // Data
in me—just—this
:

//

deep in the sweat
  of the season

tight in the hemispheres
  & bounded

by reason u dove
  of imaginary sexuality

u dimly-lit beacon of need
  of the reason u stand for

unfurled
 the plurality
of flowers
 stems bright
& pulsing
—& I am a stone.

//

//

Darwin's pond the lake
in me Orpheus

the opposite of Lethe

my hound
my sound
my skin
be bright
yr (my) flint-
knapped-
tooth,
then—

I remember

split the arrow shaft in me
grown deep | take root

the crack thru me
may yet be a wound in the earth.

//

//

O ape my arc-angelic heir
hermaphrodendritic of instinct
out|foxing the impure & imaginary light—

Lucifer, helianthus

delete, rhyme & bracken—
o ride on, virile reason—

o orchid u pensive   & dumb

//

//

the bright hysterics @ the constraints of language
"the wounds of wild animals heal quickly" : parallogic
| it does | doesn't it | heal {quickly}?—no

this haploid desire that breaks me | "forth"
is not a singular desire—

imprison'd in the open palm.

am I | are u | able—thus
a commingling—no—animal,
grovel | sugar | sugar | sweat

metalimbic echo in the drowning—hush
the bark that cracks around the tree—this pulse
lowers into us deep as a well
& as cold—

> "An angel whose muscles developed no more
> power, weight for weight, than those of an eagle
> or a pigeon would require a breast projecting for
> about four feet to house the muscles engaged in
> working its wings, while to economize in weight,
> its legs would have to be reduced to mere stilts"

what freak what monster,
this—

//

I am barely chaste
in my kilowatts tho scratched
by the joules I swallowed
2 become human, then—

.

CTRL+ALT+ESC

some trees, trumpets are
some viral, moss, is
brain stem iamb iamb share
shame if, I, eye-bright
am shall stun, owl shall
is pierce grown, here
iris-pierce, cortex-deep
like no animal, can—

I arch & absolve myself / bloody
of dawn / have sunk / sunk lower
squadron / help / stop / sing / or synch
daybite / bitch / bitten / of the song—

BRUT rosé & LASH // first thus
& ridden—sap—sucker—neck
conglomerate in excess // rush
my fault in me // hush // sweet
this—a peril in me—ask
& I will answer—gibberish—is ish
in me—& giddy / giddy / is the laughter
of doves—

O Cling—
2 the cliff in me

can sorrow be a place
if not a palace in the air,
Where—

there where the mountains rise
like teeth o Grind
them down o
sing 2 me

mottled thy spectra neon pursuit
by squirrely logic in caveat O
lapse & lithospheric strum in skin
who first a chord did thrum in
the genesis of spine | mingle
elite of nerve & twitch, recall
thy kilowatt thy irridesce
to be the body stung now of

DEEP IN THE THREAT OF INSTINCT deep in the plural aggressive there
where the storm is an iris is   sudden pleiad plead sudden alone

[plead fealty of halter   plead greedy of crown   plead hazard of
harvest   plead guilty   & come]

anapest anapest stutter & wonder   aggravate a lion—darkly—
she fed—deep in the hunted—& deep in the hidden— dactyl &
echo hunt us   instead—

give back the muscle
where an iris once bloomed
give back the weight
of a crown placed on grass

forgive us // 2 trespass // as we have // not
forgiven // genesis // this—

thy melt // thy crust // thy doom isa pink stone they that mist is
as a symphony 2 // here // is an accidental peacock

// thine sky mine eyes are, designed for // thy data thy fauna thy joy

u who curse them // diamonds cut in bark split lip o sap thy crush
is a leash to, be a lightning for // o vireo u gladiator of song

thy vulcan // thy magnolia // thy city. // thy rain, libation, come
torrential // here where everything is // u common name , u place—

not 2 worship uselessly // pearls or clouds // perilous, pendulous, not
2 hold // the sun ina wet mouth // what human nerve a bird then, flock 2

& tremble the fortress of the world // thine eyed trumpet // rim, this
deafening horizon u ride u // hide & seek

the plumage then. // thy flood // thy lisp // thy cusp // thy tilt // isa
speck caught // thy net isa eye 2, be a place for // is an urge 2

thy notes hang // thy warble warble thy croon // // thy eye then
swell then // the colors open & pour forth // vault // then release them

here // is an accidental joy // thine palace of.

I say unto u

in yr non-god filaments

most dactly & High Adonis

lake of detritus on yr face

stupid grin, moon

proud in yr manhood

nipple :: holograph ::

"not untwist"

scruff my

hypersurvival

hystericalpsychosis

heart

kinglet, my rivulet

citadel in the idiocy

come @ me

yet throb in the glucose relentless

climax   of the forest

far from the uranium   cyberskin mines

of my heart   also I google relentless Hercules & cry

juniper :: Jupiter ::   full-throttle   :: necklace

something should be made 2 apologize

in the nether regions

muscled & hairy of lilac

roll now down crevasse

& permission

against us

have u gone growling

-rod, I will make, like,   a storm in yr inner manhood

most seizure & shudder of   most xulted

instinct misdirected @ verbage

fixated on the areol & cleavage uh

of sunlight

u,

heinous apparatus

forged from the endless

I goddamn command u

in yr unspent alluvia

lake of vowels we r thrown 2

dude moon grin

proud, 2 proud 4 pearls—

my garland all spangled

can dumber sun

plenty

metadatacrunching

far from the oxygen-rich waters of my

I have flung u, little error,

I will mortify u limp

of light

man

for all this

egregious of summer

the doldrums that roll

& neck & Absolute

to Trespass

in what direction

pheromone & golden

I will cut

:: sing thine

of mother :: summer

chlorophyll

of my heart   rosaceae :: addendum ::
stupid   chordate lunatic
choir I would cut out   my tongue like a thorn
hazard a guess would you   get ground down
        by the endless wet   gizzard of the sky
        the endless grey   gauntlet of my eyes
        what my dirty hands   have touched I command u
            this is a cage & don't u   forget it :: poppy
            of yr mouth flower   of yr ceaseless urge
            is the cage of :: relentless
            thorn grown   throne bent
        under the stupid weight   of yr stupid face
        yr necklace awaits   say mercy
    say mercy mercy jilted lily   of the valley
hollow be yr stem   & hollow hollow be
    thy name   "or, most weary, cry"

92

star :: cluster :: fuck   mythic :: nimbus :: cumulative
:: spy :: phillic :: dodecagoddamnhedron :: OMFG :: I rational
skyware :: txt me alpha centauri :: blow me :: intercepted bouquet
of the rational :: poppycock :: crush :: I HAVE A CRUSH ON ::
it seems more like gravity has a crush on me :: harmosymphonical
semiquaverregretwhatever::theevolutionarysuccessofself-loathing::lol
-ing :: this earth is not weatherproof ::   phasic :: spazdic :: beautiful
banquet ::   I am singing a song can you tell what song it is :: let the
insensitive d-beat solo continue in the pulpy gonads of my heart :: kiss
me :: plz in the endless bounty :: the gazillion of things vying for
everything :: metahypersuperduperpolysaturated I lick the eyelid of the
sky :: fuck perform function :: similie is like or as I want 2 dissolve in
the forest; is a problem of temporality :: molecule ever ever :: ever after ::
wutever :: after all ::   ozone & junco & pig-skull & sustenance
& everything that has ever been :: or will come after :: me :: like a
hound :: in the endless constellation :: O Darwin :: fuck u ::
spontaneous generation :: nebula :: mingle :: elated :: Verizon
pluralizing the light IRL ugh & for ever :: I can't understand the words
of this song it just sounds like screaming ::   it's called death thrash crust
sludge doom metal for a reason :: the locust trees :: my eyes

BE PRETTY

cis. in pretty Be lucid in witness ORG is *phenomen*[o]logical [a bio(s)]
is Pierced // I put my fire in it sweet then // in excess U hunger [~~god~~] or
[~~order~~] This Plasma is suspect (*alb*—or *Solution*) reduced to the blood
is as a river // be lucid be pretty [*be viral be shine*] . U *human* in extant
xtatic in bodily [*in Boldly embodied*] where is the fear there, *Cellular*—
Mine.

swoon w. the Tidal *per-viscid* [a vesicle]—tensile & sprung w. the rampant (& springing) illicit // Synthetic—aberration is culpable // is cursive & Multiple—be hive & be swarm then [simulacra & hybrid] by raceme or Glory // flaw'd percept *"Empiric"*—clasp'd in a moment be monument by seizure be virile be volatile & clone.

Minotaur stance; *intransience a halo* is [voice] & [echo] // the hazard
has come. [re: neglect, of the halter] re: biont & *wonder* is awful
desire— pathetic // of form. *paradox* grows thorny & paws u U empty-
eyed captor [*a bird in the hand // is worth two of my own*] plead mimic
& sadness // be vetted by twilight, be adorned & alone.

THO I DO SEE

o shine ew
green u
mossy thing
@ dawn then ooze
u lightning-veined

u pond grown over
grown bold say "O"

say "ringing
-in the ears" say "each

2 each" grown
from seed the silken

grass flows across
the sun the tide

lines spume pollen foam
up the shore is breathing

my breath a million eyes stare
back across say who cares

the ground is crawling
I am a microcosm I

am a macrocosm I am a plasm a phlegm
a spasm an ache is a stitch across the surface relentless

into which a clearing opens
its endless & dizzy
fist

. . .

\ & on, as soft
-as-down grass
2 cover it, then sand,

mtns, sweep, sleep, swept
pride under sun, break me,
open, only, swear——

curse that I am a man tho I do see
& that the mirror of the puddle, sky, & trees

see me, shine blue, shine black, look back,
what glow, the mist, the dew, the grass

is blooming 2day the swarm in the light
rising off the ground, disseminate, each alight

& spinning, how could I place
anything, anywhere, with all this stuff

moving in the air // a man can stand
in one place & know nothing, nothing

even as the very ground
lurches
& swells & yields
under our
tender feet

& who cares
not me

vive, re, sir, vie, vault, alter, hiss, hive
sweet, swoon, own, earn, each, pitch, purr, loined
mythic, furtive, votive, ring, silken, swagger
any man is king, livid, ovid, vivid, sing,
lucid, answer, shelter, spring—

dim as eyes are stutter sequin'd
show the sky how eyes are lost
purse, pleasure, leisure, eon
curse the season for the frost

my vile own stars set down in stone
a limp fragrance that was my own
a swarm that swam thru buzzing air
my eyeless night a shining drone

& here & there an iris blooms
& here & there a vision looms
& here & there a owl croons

a fortress, cave, or cavern deep
can rock us in our primal sleep
revolt what volta came that day
iris, crisis, creature, stay—

sea

see sea

lair liar
lyre leer

cache cash crowned
kill kill kiss eat
creep up vine

xaog goad grunt
glee cunt put
staph rude runt

crimson eagle umbel seer
by brier scratch a sound
steel steal stole owl
don't say "mercy"

calliope lies down on dirt
I am ashamed by hurt
grief is a pink claw
constantly clawing

lay me down in an open field
liar me down unseen there
listen little creature
come closer

earth hate us earth eat us
dirt make us dirt keep us
stay stubborn steer clear
make of me a beggar, here.

PAIN SAME SHINE OR BOWER

below fear feather
come stagger forth from mingle
clasping each need sip grease sip sugar
each needs each need sun stay down go down get down roll over
uproot me be rough cut there hurt each hymn tree please

     bract braced gainst slaught
     an areol in the *slyv* lie down

purse pulse a melody want be still be still coarse radix dig me
deeper than prayer hazard wizard humble stumble dig deeper
crushed w absence crazed w dew

     sepal a lip
     sepal a cup

     vie, thistle

slipped some sudden deep & stuck in in ventricle got caught
pollute w breath just burn shun hum keep down dig deep is as able is a
need of

spring forth fallow maze in light sharp-as-a-knife my throat a throat
spoke thru be sprung be stem strung claim be stake be stroked

     font or arrow, bent
     w a fine bloom
     —rim. spadix
     be gentle,
     spathe.

THY VIRAL ORCHARDING || ESCAPE MY

i.

[

    orcharded Euridice || grown mock-sunset Ordovician
    penultimate or   is it   ultimate—

    ~~blesst~~? [ARC ARDOR ARC] ~~curst~~

    mutter muddier || fossil imprint

          got gnarly & thorny
       in stockings of mud

                      ]

] SAVE ME
] MY ANGEL
] J/K

ii.

O Polyphemos in
crimson tulle @ the
edge of the world
holding tulips

                              his gown is the color of sunset
                              his jewels are the tears of the sky
                                    weep w his one eye, O
                                       brag u of yearning
                                            oh yearn—

so who paradox | played
the lyre the first
eukaryotic dirge &
mournful anthem in the

first morning o sing me
sweetly into being into
the perversity of being I
grow muddier & more
odorous—

this rampant arc wtf
egregious in orogonies
my Ariachne digital-
modeling I cursive | am
hell-bent | will it ever
stop spinning—

cellular sonnet
whatever
in cosmic radiation
my pulpit the futile
wing
of each dead thing
forever—

::

] mammalian longing

] logical empiricism

] mitosis

] carbon bond

] subliminal violence

] rocks

}} indecency as motive

}} Mozart harvest

}} what the fuck is a holographic universe

U INCARNATION OF MOLECULAR STRUCTURE U WARM BLOODED MYTHOLOGY OF LINEAGE U MASQUERADE OF OVERDRESSED GONADS U IMAGINARY SPACESHIP ROCKETING OUTWARD U RESERVOIR OF CAPTIVE SADNESS U EVOLUTIONARY MONSTER ERUPTING FROM THE IMAGINARY FOREST, HEAR ME, UTTER, I SAY UTTER, ENTIRELY, ARGOS, EMPIRE, ANGUISH, ASPIRE, HERE IT IS, OH I AM THO EAGER EVEN, HERE, UTTERLY, TIRED, LEAVE US, SOLAR WIND, POLIS, CUMULONIMBUS, ORBITING SATELLITES, SENTIMENTALITY OF THE VERGE, MY ANGEL, PRISM, OPAL IN THE DEED, SUCCUMB HENCEFORTH, MY PERIL THIS PENDULOUS EARTH SLICK WITH OIL, O CULMINATE, MY PROTO-UTOPIA, IT SUCKS HERE, BE SIMPLE WITH LANGUAGE, DISSOLVED IN THE SATURATED LIGHT, U HYBRID U MORTAL URGENCY U BLINK & U SPILL IRREVOCABLY FORTH.

iii.

] my horns of calcite] my mountain
] my urge 2 look back] my violets
] my eyeshadow] my cowardice
] my inability to sing

pathologies of inquiry || symptoms of apples || yelling in the street
traceable lineage || neolithic love songs || who once ruled the earth
|| carcinogen || mutagenic orchard || thy fruits art // damned

iv.

PHALANX & MIRE ODE owed geo-
plasma only ugly in icon, gravel-
hearted ore or gullet, egg-
laid palm of, be a world to, a trap is,
eon & arch-eon emplaced upon,
fine then, this is, serpentine,
the layers upcurved, embedded
the vein of, is a lure to,
a fishhook in the eye of, it's my eye
I mas as well say it, the suns army
trumpets my enemy up
my enemy o my enemy the vast
legions of everything
breathing alltogether—

.

weakling eye / abutment / exoskeletonizing petal
/ lumen / want & stinger there.

.

hoarse abstract, salty-rim-of-eye, rhyme of error
geosynclinal urge more real than sonnet, tho
replication is rhyme scheme in "pure form" | admixture,
abyssal, dismal rly, then cry in the midst of, the mind of,
the don't mind me of, the churning
metadata admirroring stars.

        pulsar
   wavelength & cockstroke & spectra

admire : hox : {hoax?} fibula : altair
:oak : toad : ophiolite : photosensitivity
{non-sense & non-sensitivity}
case-sensitive & careless CGAT

adornment : mythologies : nanotech labia
microscopy : feathered antennae : mitochondria
batilions in the realm of never-night
are you awake I'm awake here
in the weird arousal of being

o electric probe & surge & residue
heir apparent "in tooth & law"
in diode & data-transfer & mega-pixel
& megalodontodont & cathedral & declaration
& magneticism & permission & grief
& harpsichord, nerves of the hand, or whatever

.

we microscope in the dew of, dawn of
we squelch & suckle; we shuck & shun
all egregious of vision ... double-focus,
triple-focus, palimpsest, enter the many,
the many-many, digi-cam & eyelid-noise
of the night-sky, so arose a rose so rose so

by bright surface receiving this globe in us the maze in me,
amazed of, there is a claw that claws the ground before me, it is
not my claw, it is not my way that stretches before me, melt the
snow before me, unfurl the leaves & gild the cliffs & bugle all
the trumpets in the never-silence, the din & whine of insects, the
endless edge that is the rim of sky, gobsmacked horizon, reflected
in each eye pried loose upon the surface, they are rolling in their
sockets, they are twitching with the ever-changing light, this is a
network, an internet, a sense particulate, we are caught of, all a
tangle there in sunlight or in the rapid shadow of the mechanism of
earth, spin, turn, turn me, over, this, gesture of form relentless, in
me, I receive you, I bear witness, give me, break me, form me, I
will yield, fawn on, universe, with yr outward appearance, u eagle
u hawk me o falcon wutever entering me, tension, touch me, the
fault is, fissure is, claw is, this is, dim but, still, I see.

NECTARIES

[]

nectaries :: has tempest :: o yellow—
o ovum & capsule :: u spaceship
2 the future :: Adonis I, mythic mightily,
ring species a crown my hell-bent absence & litany

a luxury of form. cyber-
sexual opus expanding, uncircumcised horizon
"2 which rock crystals surrender"

but never will I // yield.

[]

androidogenesis :: ultra violet wing
of metallic ions, my galaxy
ocular lasso as finch chase finch
& cache crude diatom :: pursue

the impure gonads of the first night;
mock them.

[]

my nonsense
necklace
foam

[]

globe || ransom || halter
intermediary of need
salivate, weep, whatever
shuffle || coil || seed

[]

get dome u eyelash
testicle :: flinch

[]

o nova. o blastocyst. o universe.
o rimjob of th' hopeless sun—
moon of a blank stare, stare back.

[]

barebackt in th' winter of my horizon
mumbled something or something else 2 th' wind.

[]

oh the silken internet
is lingerie 2 earths
vulgar apparatus

[]

anoint u of egret, dogwood violets teeth
pharmacological heartthrob in the cellular matrix
chemical raiment, chemosocial 2 th core
o anoint u of daydream or verb
megalodont, asterixs, (like midas but
th opposite—) survive, what wld it

take & even,
w flourish
or w
caress—

[]

this gibberish, look—

"ye mighty & despair"

is ish all like
who cares

("not me")

[]

abt yr eyes:
peel them.

u & all u touch
is made of snot
daffoldil of th sky
n all

abt yr eyes: peel them
& wash yr dirty mouth w snow

in being, be by being "fruitful, &,
Multiplicitous "

[]

shame // face of sun

I yield; I yield

[]

xtravagant finch is now

app thru 2 the constellations below my feet is now

the spinning world yields transparent

is beady in eyes & beak.

[]

roam, lucent cyborg :
hungry eyed quartzite O
lonely in hologram emblazoned mirror
of form dense w weight & urge; my animal sleeps
in the spinning eye of the universe; the milky gibberish
flung thru the sky : seek

[]

what sweetness
deep—

[]

dude, the bounty around us—
dude, the unyielding earth.

&...[]

beckon, dismal
triumph
in us

sweatglands & strata
orion might

pursue a lily
the valley, full

it is fistfuls of dimness
in us

I gather & release them

redundant of helix
& void

.

eagle-eye; talon of
pleasure & datum

& datum {datum}
{datum datum datum
datum datum}

of the hyperreal
empiricist, super-

lyrical take me
by the hand

& throw me @constellation
@becoming

this vain Vulcan
in us, mistress of eden

thrown

the depths in me Poseidon
a kings ransom in our miserable eye

.

look @ all that moss full of sorrow
but without the capacity to 2 understand sorrow

shining in the
half-
light
// why
& swan
I

stumble
heavy w. it

how fur to feathers why
to beak, to wrist
crimson, why clutch
Circe, o, mine eyes

the pileated woodpecker
of my boughs, incessant

in which I run
for cover

.

yr hogs breath all up on me & bountiful
as the pendulous boobs of the sky

THE EYE THAT I AM

i.

THRUST   THRU   OWN   SOIL   UP

WHERE IS THE AUTONOMY OF THE MEADOW

when can I lie down there

ii.

the lie is that there is order

I will make u lie down
in green pastures

will make of [our] body[s] disorder

life is a zone that inhabits

iii.

need breaks a day open & enters it

each form is bounded by matter

distinguish me from a lichen
make me stand up & answer

iv.

there has been a great mistake & we arise inside it
an eye opens it is looped to its opening

a form is an answer
to paradise looming

a form is a loom
there is no paradise

v.

zone in which the eye that I am
inhabits an elaborately constructed world

zone in which I give up
& yet fail to decompose

vi.

seraphim the sun inebriate
coiled rope ankle & neck of finch
upon the whetted throne

vii.

eye that disintegrates the various landscapes
eye that integrates the various landscapes
where we learn to distinguish
ourselves from rocks

zone in which each instant pries open its instant

the landscape holds the open eye open & enters it
where there is

neither relief nor shelter

viii.

all held at order, whole landscapes of tension
whole landscapes hold themselves erect

whole legions of trees—
each minute scale & fibre—

it is too much

ix.

"forc't hallelujahs"

x.

in which the universe relentlessly invents an eye
it insists on it incessantly:: vanity; or necessity "to be seen"

I WILL MAKE U LIE DOWN

I WILL MAKE U TROUBLE THE WATERS

I WILL PUNISH & BRING FORTH THE SPRING

AN EYE IS A TOOL IT SUBMITS TO THE EARTH

I WILL PLOW U W CLOVER & REAP U

xi.

the iris contracts w fear

xii.

a pond blinks when a cloud passes over

xiii.

in my answer there is not even the seed of a small thing

WIZARD ERRONEOUS OF BLUE-BELL SILVER-MINNOW-FLASH A POOL IN ME BY DISASTROUS OF NETS IS CAUGHT IN ME A MONSTER LIZARD OF MY BRAIN-STEM OF MY CHORDATE INNER EYE MERCILESS I YIELD I YIELD

BY GAZE

by gaze inhabit
thy motion only

shock sky w nakedness shock
mountain w unforgiven – animal

of my animal throw
geese into the sky
by their throats this
world is unforgiven.

unangel me in darkness
unangel the darkness
meat eat meat turn
into it as the day turns

into dimness a choir of
howls resounds in the hills

hills flooded with sunlight
hills hollowed by sunlight
trees are hollow they are a thin
membrane around their discarded cores.

***

the motile stirring Dawn hurt
is error "to wander"
 || shock stunted winter

a "clean break" be
guilty, storm, as shale
flaked sky from calm;
corrosive breath

& yet built a body of.
|| petulant &
boggy ravine all
"glistering" w frost

& dead the endless
procession & dead the
piles on the earth & dead
the marshgrass & dead
the prariegrass & dead the
downed dead trees
the trunks bent under,
snapped & frayed in death

weighed down w the weight
of the xcellent & living excess

***

musk-grape, mammal eye,
nerve end, fat deposit,
green-blue, pair bond,
canine, blue-bell,
pig-sty, sunlight
prairie grass, mountain-ash
solemnly, root-bud
scent-gland, taste-bud,
fire-lily, snow-lily,
choke-hold, day-break
minds-eye, worlds-end
mucous membrane, salt.

a mirror a silver'd iris a tigers-eye
stalk is beat tho prey be fast
the wind a shook thing, the raining down
the tall trees bow down, glory
be to all that needs. wait,
wait tho clutch & crouch &
wait, lithe feet
be beat-
en path thru
cyclic
leaves
as trace
make
day

make
day
marked
by break.

Ash,
bend.
Lily,
bend.
hand,
leg, foot,
lip,
bend.

break,
day, each
to each
bend broken,
back.

glory
glory
glory
little creature
proto-eye
& hidden,
then
be as snow-
melt, each
day, be

warm,
blooded
honey-
suckl'd
salt.

***

by day, reap
by night, reap,
dream, grim,
reap what thrush
-hearted grain
giddy
w reaping.

by day, wait
by day, gaze
into the next
be steady, hold
steady.

giddy, horse-
of-my-horse, hours
tread hours till,
flushed, dominion—

swept grass marks circles
in wind on sand, debris marks
tides, is washed by tides, nest
of my nest, day

tread day by light
forgot what light
might need,
need sight—

give back
a prism
there, by
gaze is
gaze met

to reap
each day
is days
price.

// be corrupt in xchange :: is gem is copy, swapped
thin membrane, mucus is nest then // hustle // to eat
is born anew || replica // replicata // mingled, elated
by noise. mimic enter. mimic war. anoxic, is permeable, shore.

mock animal what small sensation. self as secretion
be as if // impelled // bilateral— diurnal, nocturnal, arhythmic
& yet rhythmic; own, owned or otherwise is an oil-droplet
is a fragment of a moment, flee.

nothing is formless. all is aggregate // all is gated // gutted
glutted w being & hungry w being & sore.

save by a thin wall, a cell, begotten by being got
by being eaten, enmeshed in marsh or swamp of being
held, beheld, beaten into some semblance of submission
each hour erected where wrecked, in wreckage, born.

grown sea-beast of cold waters
ashamed by hem & tide
cleave, calm gaze of morning
shed [thy] gaze &
shed thy dress
of foam

spilt sepal & milky o'er orion
as the waves rise up
& as the mist off the waves
& as the sky rise up
& o'er the glare
another glare
glares up

//

the hum comes sudden
low. there is a wept in the distance.
there is a massive distance between us.
thigh, sing tide, grow petal, dim
in anchor, cursive spine. green
thing, eat sun. peel me salt
as a gown sloughed off,
as avalanche & storm.

nether, tether, thither, asunder
ass-under neither I nor I
in excess, be but thrown from it
gelding, glimmer
in the eye in the eye
of a storm.

hurt hunt, heat eat heat
eat me make a mess
of the day

come tomorrow, all this "open" will be
overgrown.

ABOUT THE AUTHOR

CODY-ROSE CLEVIDENCE lives in the Arkansas Ozarks with their dog, pearl. Their first book, *Beast Feast,* also from Ahsahta, was a finalist for the 2016 CLMP Firecracker Award in poetry and their little chapbook, *Perverse, All Monstrous,* is newly out from Nion Editions.

AHSAHTA PRESS
NEW SERIES

AHSAHTA PRESS

SAWTOOTH POETRY PRIZE SERIES

2002: Aaron McCollough, *Welkin* (Brenda Hillman, judge)

2003: Graham Foust, *Leave the Room to Itself* (Joe Wenderoth, judge)

2004: Noah Eli Gordon, *The Area of Sound Called the Subtone* (Claudia Rankine, judge)

2005: Karla Kelsey, *Knowledge, Forms, The Aviary* (Carolyn Forché, judge)

2006: Paige Ackerson-Kiely, *In No One's Land* (D. A. Powell, judge)

2007: Rusty Morrison, *the true keeps calm biding its story* (Peter Gizzi, judge)

2008: Barbara Maloutas, *the whole Marie* (C. D. Wright, judge)

2009: Julie Carr, *100 Notes on Violence* (Rae Armantrout, judge)

2010: James Meetze, *Dayglo* (Terrance Hayes, judge)

2011: Karen Rigby, *Chinoiserie* (Paul Hoover, judge)

2012: T. Zachary Cotler, *Sonnets to the Humans* (Heather McHugh, judge)

2013: David Bartone, *Practice on Mountains* (Dan Beachy-Quick, judge)

2014: Aaron Apps, *Dear Herculine* (Mei-mei Berssenbrugge, judge)

2015: Vincent Toro, *Stereo. Island. Mosaic.* (Ed Roberson, judge)

2016: Jennifer Nelson, *Civilization Makes Me Lonely* (Anne Boyer, judge)

2017: Jonah Mixon-Webster, *Stereo[TYPE]* (Tyrone Williams, judge)

This book is set in Apollo MT type
with DIN Light titles
by Ahsahta Press at Boise State University.
Cover design by Quemadura.
Book design by Janet Holmes.

AHSAHTA PRESS
2018

JANET HOLMES, DIRECTOR

LINDSEY APPELL
PATRICIA BOWEN, *intern*
MICHAEL GREEN
KATHRYN JENSEN
COLIN JOHNSON
MATT NAPLES